DOING MARRIAGE GOD'S WAY

THE FOUNDATIONS

GROUP PARTICIPANT GUIDE

JIMMY EVANS

DOING MARRIAGE GOD'S WAY

THE FOUNDATIONS

GROUP PARTICIPANT GUIDE

JIMMY EVANS

XO
PUBLISHING

XO
PUBLISHING

Doing Marriage God's Way: The Foundations: Group Participant Guide
Copyright © 2025 by Jimmy Evans

ISBN: 978-1-960870-63-6 eBook
ISBN: 978-1-960870-64-3 Paperback

XO Publishing is a leading creator of relationship-based resources. We focus primarily on marriage-related content for churches, small group curriculum, and people looking for timeless truths about relationships and overall marital health. For more information on other resources from XO Publishing, visit XOPublishing.com.

XO Publishing
1021 Grace Lane
Southlake, TX 76092

While the authors make every effort to provide accurate URLs at the time of printing for external or third-party internet websites, neither they nor the publisher assume any responsibility for changes or errors made after publication.

Printed in the United States of America

25 26 27 28—5 4 3 2 1

Table of Contents

Introduction

Welcome!

Welcome to *Doing Marriage God's Way: The Foundations!* Over the next six sessions, you'll discover the biblical foundations that make every successful marriage work. This manual is your personal workbook for reflection, activities, and application.

HOW TO USE THIS MANUAL:

- Bring this manual to every session.
- Complete reflection exercises during your personal time.
- Use the spaces provided for notes during video teaching.
- Be honest in your assessments—growth requires honesty.
- Apply the homework consistently for best results.

GROUP GUIDELINES:

- What's shared here, stays here (practice confidentiality).
- Speak for yourself, not your spouse.
- Listen to understand, not to give advice.
- Honor different perspectives and marriage seasons.
- Focus on growth, not perfection.

SESSION 1

The Most Important Decision in Marriage

KEY SCRIPTURE

Jesus answered and said to her, "Whoever drinks of this water will thirst again, but whoever drinks of the water that I shall give him will never thirst. But the water that I shall give him will become in him a fountain of water springing up into everlasting life."

—John 4:13–14

VIDEO TEACHING NOTES

- The four deepest human needs are: _____, _____, _____, and _____.
- **Acceptance** means I need someone to accept me for _____ I really am.
- **Identity** means I need to know _____ I am.
- **Security** means I need to be truly _____.
- **Purpose** means I need to know _____ I'm here.
- The principle of _____ says: When I don't trust God to meet my deepest needs, I immediately transfer the expectation to my _____.
- _____ is a personal relationship with Jesus Christ.

PERSONAL REFLECTION: THE FOUR DEEPEST NEEDS

For each need, circle where you *currently* look to get it met:

IDENTITY (Who am I?)

- Spouse's opinion
- Job performance
- Children's success
- Others' approval
- God's truth about me

ACCEPTANCE (Am I loved?)

- Spouse's affection
- Friends' inclusion
- Family approval
- Social media likes
- God's unconditional love

SECURITY (Am I safe?)

- Financial status
- Spouse's mood
- Health conditions
- Circumstances
- God's faithfulness

PURPOSE (Do I matter?)

- Career success
- Others' praise
- Spouse's appreciation
- Achievements
- God's calling on my life

REFLECTION QUESTIONS

1. Which of the four needs do you most often look to your spouse to fulfill?

   _____

2. How has trying to get your spouse to meet your deepest needs affected your marriage?

   _____

3. What would change in your marriage if your deepest needs were anchored in Jesus?

   _____

4. What specific step can you take this week to develop your personal relationship with Jesus?

   _____

THIS WEEK'S APPLICATION

- ☐ Spend time in prayer each morning, bringing your deepest needs to Jesus.
- ☐ Have a conversation with your spouse about the principle of transference.
- ☐ Commit to daily quiet time with God before engaging with your spouse.

NOTES

_____

_____

_____

_____

_____

_____

_____

_____

_____

_____

_____

_____

_____

_____

_____

_____

_____

_____

_____

SESSION 2

The Law of Priority

Leaving and Cleaving

Therefore a man shall leave his father and mother and be joined to his wife, and they shall become one flesh.

—Genesis 2:24

VIDEO TEACHING NOTES

- The four laws of marriage come from Genesis chapter _____,
  _____ verses and _____.
- The first law of marriage is the law of _____.
- The word "leave" means to _____.
- Your marriage has to come _____ in your life, except for your relationship with _____.
- Most things that destroy marriages aren't _____ things—they're just _____ things out of priority.
- The way you establish value is: What are you willing to _____ for me?
- Legitimate _____ means "I created you for me first, and I don't like it when you give my love somewhere else."

PRIORITY AUDIT

Weekly Time Allocation

(Average hours per week):

- Work: _____ hours
- Spouse (focused attention): _____ hours
- Children: _____ hours
- TV/Entertainment: _____ hours
- Social Media: _____ hours
- Hobbies: _____ hours
- Exercise: _____ hours
- Friends: _____ hours

Priority Check Questions

Check all that apply:

- ☐ My spouse gets my best energy, not leftovers.
- ☐ I put my phone away when my spouse is talking.
- ☐ I prioritize my spouse's needs over others' requests.
- ☐ My spouse feels like they come first in my life.

PERSONAL REFLECTION QUESTIONS

1. What currently competes with your spouse for first place in your priorities?

   _____

2. What would you need to give up or reorganize to put your spouse first?

   _____

3. How have your children (if applicable) taken priority over your marriage?

   _____

4. What specific action can you take this week to demonstrate that your spouse comes first?

   _____

THIS WEEK'S APPLICATION

☐ Identify one thing you need to "hang up" (like Jimmy's golf clubs) to prioritize your spouse.

☐ Schedule one hour of uninterrupted, face-to-face time with your spouse.

☐ Put your phone away during all conversations with your spouse.

NOTES

_____

_____

_____

_____

_____

_____

_____

_____

_____

_____

_____

_____

_____

_____

_____

_____

_____

SESSION 3

The Law of Pursuit

Working at Love

KEY SCRIPTURE

"[A]nd the two shall become one flesh'; so then they are no longer two, but one flesh."

—Mark 10:8

VIDEO TEACHING NOTES

- The word "cleave" or "be joined to" means to pursue with all of your _____.
- You fell in love because you _____ at the relationship.
- You fall out of love because you _____ working at the relationship.
- Marriage only works when you _____ at it.
- We get married because we _____ meet our own needs.
- The question "Are you _____?" means: If there's anything I'm not doing, or if there's a need in you that I'm not meeting, I will do whatever it takes to make sure it's taken care of.
- In relationships, _____ are the engine and _____ are the caboose in an unhealthy relationship. This should be reversed.
- If you do the _____ thing, you'll feel the _____ feelings.

PURSUIT ASSESSMENT

Rate yourself honestly (1–10):

- I actively pursue my spouse: _____/10
- I am sensitive to my spouse's needs: _____/10
- I work daily at our relationship: _____/10
- I prioritize meeting my spouse's needs: _____/10

PERSONAL REFLECTION QUESTIONS

1. In what ways have you become "lazy" in your marriage?

   _____

2. What needs of your spouse have you been ignoring or minimizing?

   _____

3. How can you pursue your spouse this week in a way that matters to them?

   _____

4. What daily disciplines do you need to establish to keep love alive in your marriage?

   _____

DAILY PURSUIT PLAN

Write three specific ways you will pursue your spouse this week:

1. _____

2. _____

3. _____

THIS WEEK'S APPLICATION

- ☐ Ask your spouse daily: "Are you okay? Is there anything you need?"
- ☐ Schedule and protect one hour of face-to-face communication daily.
- ☐ Plan and execute a meaningful date night.
- ☐ Take care of yourself physically (appearance, hygiene, health).

NOTES

SESSION 4

The Law of Partnership

Becoming One

KEY SCRIPTURE

"... and they shall become one flesh."

—Genesis 2:24

VIDEO TEACHING NOTES

- The third law of marriage is the law of _____.
- "One flesh" refers to _____ union, but also means we're _____.
- In Genesis chapters 1 and 2, there's never a reference to Adam being _____ Eve or Eve being _____ Adam.
- God didn't create marriage to be _____ for one person to rule over the other.
- Dominance is _____ neutral—there are just as many dominant females as dominant males.
- Marriage is a corporation where you both own ____% of the stock.
- Everything has _____ names on it: yours, your spouse's, and _____.
- The word "my" _____ relationships. It should always be "our."
- Colossians 3 tells us to let the _____ of Christ rule our hearts. The word "rule" means to _____.

15

PARTNERSHIP ASSESSMENT

Check areas where you function well as a team:

- ☐ Financial decisions
- ☐ Parenting choices
- ☐ Social calendar
- ☐ Household responsibilities
- ☐ Major purchases
- ☐ Career decisions
- ☐ Extended family relationships

Areas where we need to improve partnership:

_____

_____

_____

_____

DOMINANCE CHECK

Check all that apply:

- ☐ I make major decisions without consulting my spouse.
- ☐ I control the finances.
- ☐ I use "my" more than "our" (my car, my money, my kids).
- ☐ I expect my spouse to accept my decisions.
- ☐ I become defensive when my spouse questions my choices.
- ☐ I believe my opinion matters more in certain areas.

PERSONAL REFLECTION QUESTIONS

1. In what areas of your marriage do you tend to be dominant or controlling?

   _____

2. What things in your home have only your name on them (not shared equally)?

   _____

3. How does your spouse feel about major decisions in your home?

   _____

4. What would need to change for you to be true equal partners?

   _____

THIS WEEK'S APPLICATION

- ☐ Pray together about one major decision you need to make.
- ☐ Discuss and agree on a spending limit that requires mutual agreement.
- ☐ Have a conversation about areas where one person feels excluded from decisions.
- ☐ Practice waiting for peace from both spouses before making any major decision.

NOTES

SESSION 5

The Law of Purity

Creating Safety

KEY SCRIPTURE

And they were both naked, the man and his wife, and were not ashamed.

—Genesis 2:25

VIDEO TEACHING NOTES

- The fourth law of marriage is the law of _____.
- The word "naked" (arum) means _____.
- Adam and Eve were physically, mentally, emotionally, and spiritually totally _____, and they felt no fear or shame.
- After they sinned, they _____ their nakedness and felt _____.
- Who told you that you were naked? Answer: When you sin, you open yourself up to _____, who whispers that you're _____.
- "Death and life are in the power of the _____."—Proverbs 18:21
- Pastor Jimmy devastated Karen with his _____ for the first three years of their marriage.
- When Pastor Jimmy started taking _____ for his behavior, their marriage was transformed.
- The wages of sin _____ death (not was, not will be—IS death).
- Sin_____to us and makes us feel_____and_____.
- Taking responsibility means saying: "I'm _____. I was _____. Will you _____ me?"

19

PURITY ASSESSMENT

Rate your "safety level" in these areas (1–10):

- My spouse feels safe to share thoughts honestly: _____/10
- My spouse feels safe to be emotionally vulnerable: _____/10
- My spouse feels safe to be physically open: _____/10
- I take responsibility when I hurt my spouse: _____/10

FIG LEAF INVENTORY

What "fig leaves" (protective barriers) exist in your marriage?

Check all that apply:

- ☐ Withholding honest thoughts
- ☐ Avoiding emotional vulnerability
- ☐ Sexual withdrawal or disconnection
- ☐ Hiding behind humor or sarcasm
- ☐ Staying busy to avoid deep conversation
- ☐ Using children as buffers
- ☐ Financial secrecy

PERSONAL REFLECTION QUESTIONS

1. In what ways have you sinned against your spouse that you haven't taken responsibility for?

   _____

2. How have you used your words to hurt rather than heal your spouse?

   _____

3. What behaviors create an unsafe environment in your marriage?

   _____

4. What would it take for you to be "naked and unashamed" with your spouse?

   _____

THIS WEEK'S APPLICATION

☐ Identify one way you've sinned against your spouse and apologize specifically.

☐ Practice saying: "I'm sorry. I was wrong. Will you forgive me?"

☐ Have a conversation about what makes each of you feel safe or unsafe.

☐ Remove one "fig leaf" by being vulnerable in an area you usually hide.

NOTES

God's Blueprint

His Design for Husbands and Wives

KEY SCRIPTURE

> "... submitting to one another in the fear of God."
>
> —Ephesians 5:21

VIDEO TEACHING NOTES

- Ephesians chapter _____ is the most revelatory text any-where in the Bible about marriage.
- The husband's role: _____ servant leader
- The wife's role: _____ helpmate
- The most profound need that women have is _____.
- The most profound need that men have is _____.
- Nothing makes a woman feel more secure than a _____, _____ man.
- Nothing makes a woman feel more insecure than a _____, _____ man.
- Adam's sin in the garden was _____ (doing nothing while Satan tempted Eve).
- Eve's sin in the garden was _____ (acting without talking to God or Adam).
- The relational sin of women is believing they don't need their _____ and can act _____ of him.
- The relational sin of men is _____ and being checked out.
- Ephesians 5 says _____ as much to men as it says to women.
- The standard for wives: Would you _____ that to Jesus?
- The standard for husbands: Love your wife as you would your own _____.

ROLE ASSESSMENT

For Wives:

Rate yourself (1–10):

- I honor my husband in my words and actions: ____/10
- I include my husband in decisions: ____/10
- I respect my husband's leadership: ____/10
- I would treat Jesus the way I treat my husband: ____/10

For Husbands:

Rate yourself (1–10):

- I sacrifice my preferences for my wife: ____/10
- I actively serve my wife: ____/10
- I make my wife feel secure: ____/10
- I love my wife as I love my own body: ____/10

SIN NATURE CHECK

For Wives:

Check areas of independence that need to be surrendered:

- ☐ Making decisions without consulting husband
- ☐ Dismissing husband's input or feelings
- ☐ Acting as if I don't need my husband
- ☐ Speaking disrespectfully about my husband
- ☐ Taking control instead of partnering

For Husbands:

Check areas of apathy that need to be confronted:

- ☐ Being passive in decision-making
- ☐ Failing to protect my wife emotionally
- ☐ Not initiating spiritual leadership
- ☐ Being detached or distant
- ☐ Failing to fight for our marriage

PERSONAL REFLECTION QUESTIONS

1. How does your sin nature (independence for wives, apathy for husbands) show up in your marriage?

   _____

2. What specific actions demonstrate your role as defined in Ephesians 5?

   _____

3. How does fulfilling your biblical role meet your spouse's deepest need?

   _____

4. What one change would most improve how you fulfill your role in marriage?

   _____

THIS WEEK'S APPLICATION

- ☐ Read Ephesians 5:21-33 together and discuss what stands out.
- ☐ **Wives:** Practice honoring your husband in one specific way daily.
- ☐ **Husbands:** Practice sacrificial love by serving your wife in one specific way daily.
- ☐ **Both:** Identify one sin nature pattern and commit to change.

NOTES

_____

_____

_____

_____

_____

_____

_____

_____

_____

_____

_____

_____

_____

_____

_____

_____

_____

_____

_____

Course Review

Living Out the Foundations

THE FOUR LAWS OF MARRIAGE (Genesis 2:24–25)

1. **Law of Priority**—Marriage must come first (except for God)
2. **Law of Pursuit**—Work energetically at your relationship
3. **Law of Partnership**—Treat each other as equal partners
4. **Law of Purity**—Take responsibility for your behavior

THE FOUNDATION

First Priority:

Trust Jesus with your four deepest needs (acceptance, identity, security, purpose) before expecting your spouse to meet them.

Biblical Roles:

- Husbands: Sacrificial servant leaders
- Wives: Respectful helpmates
- Both: Submit to one another out of reverence for Christ

BIGGEST TAKEAWAYS

What are the three most important things you've learned in this course?

1. _____

2. _____

3. _____

30-DAY ACTION PLAN

Choose your top priority from the course and create a specific plan:

My Priority:

(Circle one)

- Daily Time with Jesus
- Law of Priority
- Law of Pursuit
- Law of Partnership
- Law of Purity
- Biblical Roles

Why this is my priority?

_____

Daily Action:

I will _____ .

Weekly Action:

I will _____ .

Accountability:

I will check in with _____ .

Marriage Vision

Complete this statement together with your spouse:

"With God's help, we commit to building our marriage on these foundations. We will trust Jesus with our deepest needs, follow the four laws of marriage, and fulfill our biblical roles. Our marriage will be marked by..."

_____

_____

_____

_____

_____

_____

_____

_____

_____

_____

_____

Signatures:

Husband: _____ Date: _____

Wife: _____ Date: _____

Final Encouragement

You don't have to be perfect—just committed to growing together. Use these foundations consistently, extend grace to each other often, and remember that God is for your marriage. When you build on these biblical foundations, you can have the marriage God designed you to have.

> Unless the Lord builds the house,
> They labor in vain who build it;
> Unless the Lord guards the city,
> The watchman stays awake in vain.
>
> —Psalm 127:1